Francis Willey Kelsey

The Presbyterian Church and the University of Michigan

An address before the Synod of Michigan at Adrian, October 9, 1895

Francis Willey Kelsey

The Presbyterian Church and the University of Michigan
An address before the Synod of Michigan at Adrian, October 9, 1895

ISBN/EAN: 9783337035761

Printed in Europe, USA, Canada, Australia, Japan

Cover: Foto ©Lupo / pixelio.de

More available books at **www.hansebooks.com**

Published as a Supplement to the "Michigan Presbyterian," Aug. 13, 1896

THE

PRESBYTERIAN CHURCH

AND THE

University of Michigan

AN ADDRESS BEFORE THE SYNOD OF MICHIGAN AT ADRIAN, OCTOBER 9, 1895

By FRANCIS W. KELSEY

Professor of Latin in the University

WITH STATISTICAL TABLES AND OTHER DATA

By DELOS F. WILCOX

Fellow in the Columbia College School of Political Science. New York

BY ORDER OF THE SYNOD OF MICHIGAN
1895

PREFATORY NOTE.

The following address was given before the Synod of Michigan at the request of several persons interested in the work at Ann Arbor, and is published by order of the Synod. (See the Minutes of Synod, 1895, p. 27.) The statistical tables and other data collected by Mr. Wilcox, which were laid before the Synod only in part, are printed in full and placed together for convenience of reference; they are intended to be a contribution to scientific educational literature, to present facts without reference to their bearing. Foot-notes have been added containing references to sources, or fuller information, where such seemed to be needed. Mention of indebtedness is due to Professor William H. Pettee, of the University of Michigan, for kind assistance in verifying the statistics.

FRANCIS W. KELSEY.

Ann Arbor, Michigan.
10 March, 1896.

CONTENTS

THE PRESBYTERIAN CHURCH

AND THE

UNIVERSITY OF MICHIGAN.

THE PRESBYTERIAN STUDENTS AT THE UNIVERSITY.

A calling-list of Presbyterian students at the University of Michigan, compiled by the student-secretary of the Tappan Presbyterian Association in the earlier part of the college year 1894-95, contained 401 names.[1] This list, while exact as far as it went, was not complete even for the quarter in which it was made; had it been complete it could not be taken as accurately representing the attendance of Presbyterian students for the whole year, because not including accessions of new students between the Christmas vacation and the following July.

In 1892-93 a partial religious census of the students at the University was taken by the Students' Christian Association.[2] Out of 2,808 students in attendance 487 were not reached by the census-takers; among the 2,321, or nearly six-sevenths of the entire number, whose religious preferences were ascertained, 407 Presbyterian students were registered.

It is the unanimous opinion of the men best able to judge of this matter that 475 is a conservative estimate of the number

---

[1] See Table I., p 28.

[2] See Tables XI.-XIV., pp 42-43 The difficulty of taking a complete religious census will be understood when one considers not only the magnitude of the task, but also the fact that it has not been possible to set aside funds for the purpose; the data were gathered by students whose time was quite fully occupied with their University work.

of Presbyterian students at the University the past year; that a complete census, including church members and those of Presbyterian preference, would probably have shown a somewhat greater figure than this; and that, therefore, the number 475 may be taken as a fair and accurate basis of computation.[3] In the following remarks I shall make no reference to the Presbyterian students from out of town in the Ann Arbor High School, nor to those enrolled in the University School of Music. In comparing the attendance at other institutions, fairness requires that in each case only those students be counted together who have their work on the same campus, and that preparatory as well as music and art pupils be excluded. What, then, is the meaning of the figures given?

In the first place, it is clear that one student out of every six in the University of Michigan is to be reckoned as belonging to the Presbyterian denomination by actual membership or by affiliation.

In the second place, a moment's consideration will show that the second largest Presbyterian college in the United States, in point of attendance, is at Ann Arbor. In 1894-95 the total enrollment of students in the College of New Jersey at Princeton was 1,109; next comes the Presbyterian student body at Ann Arbor with 475. Of the students at Princeton about one-half, say 555, were Presbyterian.[4] That is to say, the number of Presbyterian students at Princeton last year exceeded the number

---

[3] According to present indications, the number of Presbyterian students the present year (1895-96) will exceed 500.

[4] Extract from a letter written by Clinton T. Wood, General Secretary of the Philadelphian Society of Princeton College, 15 October, 1895: "There are no statistics of the Junior and Sophomore classes at hand. A justifiable estimate can be made, however, on the basis of the reports from the Senior and Freshman classes. Of a senior class of 260, about 130 are adherents of the Presbyterian church. Of the 280 new men we have reports of 135 who are Presbyterian adherents, and some few not reported. Of the 135, more than 100 are church members."

of Presbyterian students at Ann Arbor by barely 80. At Princeton, says Mr. Wood, "the remainder are divided among the Episcopal, Methodist, Baptist and Reformed and Congregational churches, with the larger number connected with the Episcopal church." At Ann Arbor there is a contingent of students who, having no church connections or affiliations, occasionally come to the Presbyterian church and attend the social gatherings of the Young People's Society. In the course of last year sixty-seven such voluntarily presented their names, and they were only a portion of the whole number. In final computation it is extremely probable that the number of students at Ann Arbor the spiritual welfare of whom, with absolute exclusion of all thought of proselyting, may properly be deemed a matter of concern to the Presbyterian church, is fully as great as at Princeton, or even greater.

But there are other colleges besides Princeton which our church, in her literature and through pulpit utterances, holds up before men as her contribution to the educational forces of our country. How many students do they reach? Lafayette, with all the enthusiasm of a new and vigorous regime, had last year but 306, about five-eighths the number of Presbyterian students at Ann Arbor. Hamilton, the pride of our church in New York State, had last year 141 students, less than one-third of the number of Presbyterian students at the University of Michigan. But what of the better established colleges further west, to which our church points with so much satisfaction and hope? Count them together on the statistical basis mentioned:

University of Wooster, in Ohio, with 244 students.

Wabash College, in Indiana, with 157 students.

Hanover College, in Indiana, with 110 students.

Lake Forest College, in Illinois, with 122 students.

Parsons College, in Iowa, with 100 students,

and you have, all told, in the five strongest Presbyterian educational institutions between the Great Lakes and the Rocky Mountains, 733 resident students of collegiate rank, about one and one-half as many as the Presbyterian students on the campus at Ann Arbor. Further, suppose that we unite, at some intermediate point, Hamilton, with its decades of tradition and wide influence, and Lake Forest College, with its high standard and abundant promise; we find but 263 students in attendance last year, less than two-thirds the number of Presbyterian students at the University of Michigan. Cast into one common college Wabash and Hanover and Parsons, and you have but 367 students, a little more than three-fourths the number of Presbyterian students at Ann Arbor.

There is also a group of institutions which the Presbyterian church has taken under her mantle through the Board of Aid for Colleges and Academics. In this group are 22 institutions, which last year enrolled a total of 588 students of collegiate rank, or a little more than 26 Collegiate students apiece. For these students the church, through the Board of Aid and direct contributions, expended an average of $18.28 each,[5] or a total of $10,748.84. Nearly $11,000 expended for the spiritual care and training of 588 advanced students in twenty-two institutions. Truly a noble work! Yet here are aggregated in one center, so that they can be gathered in a single hall and reached by the sound of a single voice, nearly as many of the church's own children, left, so far as the church at large is concerned, as sheep having no shepherd.

WHY DOES THE CHURCH NEGLECT HER OWN?

I have heard but two reasons assigned for the indifference of the Presbyterian church to the spiritual interests of the aggregation of Presbyterian students at the University of Michigan, an aggregation which in some respects has no parallel elsewhere.

---

[5] Total contributions (average $32.78), $19,274.64. See Table II., p. 29.

The first is that the University of Michigan does not send forth ministers, and that, as the rearing of an educated and efficient ministry is the first aim of denominational institutions, the church has no ground of direct interest in a State University whose students go into other walks of life. What are the facts in the case? Mr. Delos F. Wilcox, a graduate student of the University of Michigan and a trained investigator, last year devoted much time for six months to collecting and arranging data bearing upon the question, What has the University of Michigan done in the way of educating ministers and missionaries? In connection with this work, he investigated the religious and moral tendencies of the university life from the beginning down to the present. The statistical tables prepared by him speak for themselves. Interesting as many of the data are, it is impossible here to comment on them, or to treat them in detail. These facts, however, stand out with almost startling distinctness:

1. That in the half century ending in 1894 the University of Michigan sent out at least 299 clergymen and missionaries, an average of about six for each graduating class.[6]

2. That the ratio of ministers to the classical male graduates declined from 24.1 per cent in the decade 1845-1854 to 5.9 per cent in the decade 1875-1884; that the decade 1885-1894 shows a marked increase, from 5.9 per cent to 8.3 per cent. Attention is here directed to the fact that in this decade the organization of the Tappan Presbyterian Association falls, which began to occupy McMillan Hall in 1891;[7] that in this same period come the development of the Episcopal guild work at Harris

---

[6]See Table X., p. 40.

[7]Note the percentages of Table IV., p. 37.

1890, 2.8 per cent. of classical graduates entered the ministry.
1891, 10.2 per cent. of classical graduates entered the ministry.
1892, 8.9 per cent. of classical graduates entered the ministry.
1893, 10.2 per cent of classical graduates entered the ministry.
1894, 15.2 per cent. of classical graduates entered the ministry.

Hall, and, more recently still, the organization of the Wesleyan Guild, which is already inaugurating measures for the care of the Methodist students.

3. That of the classical graduates who entered the ministry in the classes from 1845-1880, thirty-eight, nearly one-fourth of the whole number, became Presbyterian clergymen.

These facts seem to me to show conclusively that on the whole the proportion of graduates entering the ministry from the University of Michigan has been smaller than is desirable, to keep the balance between the learned professions. But the reasons why this is true are not far to seek. First, young men who intend to study for the ministry are naturally enough urged to go to denominational institutions; and those who are attracted to the University of Michigan by the range of its curriculum are often obliged to run the gauntlet of dissuasion on the part of denominational friends. Again, the university extends no privileges to ministerial students in the way of free tuition and scholarships provided for them by the liberality of donors. In the third place, the subject of the ministry, as a calling, is not set before the students so constantly and so prominently as in many, by no means all, denominational institutions. In certain of these, as we all know, a kind of pressure often forces into the ministry, as along the line of least resistance, men without enough of either brains or consecration to do effective religious work. I have known such to be carried along on scholarship funds only to be a drag on the church after they entered the work, usually becoming soured, sooner or later, because thinking that the church and the world owed them a living which they somehow failed to get. Such institutions as these are at one extreme; the larger state universities are, from the nature of the case, at the other. With the present attitude of the

---

Presbyterian church toward the state universities[8] the wonder is, not that the University of Michigan sends so few into the Presbyterian ministry, but that it ever sends any at all.[9]

The second reason for the church's neglect is to be found in a feeling, more general in the east than in the west, that the State University is only a temporary affair, which will be politely but decisively bowed out of existence by the denominational institutions when these shall have become stronger and richer; and that its decline will be rapid and sure in the measure that its activities are either scrupulously ignored by denominational leaders, or visited with sweeping condemnation. It needs no words of mine, in this presence, to refute the belief, now held by very few, that the University of Michigan is in any special sense the source of evil tendencies. The moral tone of its student life is just as high as that of any other institution of somewhere near equal numbers.[10] To be specific, so far as I have been able to judge from various lines of evidence, it is just as high as that of Yale or of Princeton. In matters of this kind it is necessary not to let prejudice, or induction from insufficient data, warp our conclusions. When, as a student, I for the first time met students from an eastern Presbyterian college, there was a party of six; and of these three became intoxicated before they returned. Should I on that account indulge in charges against the high standards of conduct and strong discipline that have always been characteristic of that college? When the life at Ann Arbor has been spoken against I have found it expedient to inquire how many students the critic has personally known, or known on sound evidence, to have been misled because of

---

[9]"It is an encouraging fact," says Professor R. T. Ely (in The Kingdom, 7 June, 1895), "that in the State University of Minnesota there have been in recent years relatively more students who intended to enter the ministry than in Yale College."

[10]Interesting testimony regarding religious conditions at the University of Michigan may be found in an article on "A Working University," by Gertrude Buck, in The Golden Rule for 16 January, 1896.

their attendance at the University of Michigan. Probably there are some weak or vicious young men that go astray at all institutions, small as well as great. On the other hand, if personal observation is of any value, there is a considerable proportion of men who have overcome their vicious tendencies at the University and have gone out stronger morally and religiously, as well as intellectually, than when they entered.[11] If the remarks formerly often, now rarely made about the moral tone of student life at the University of Michigan were true, how has it happened that in all these years, with so many young ladies at the University, away from home and mingling freely with young men, no one has ever dared to point the finger of accusation at a University woman student? Surely, had they been well-founded, nothing less than the direct and constant intervention of an overruling Providence could have prevented scandals. But if the influences at the University of Michigan were as bad as they have occasionally been represented to be, would it be the duty of a great religious denomination to try to remedy the evil, or to gather up the folds of its garments and with averted face

---

[11] By reference to Tables XI., XII., (pp. 42-43), it will be seen that in the year 1892-93, 50.9 per cent. of all the men, 75.2 per cent. of all the women among the 2,321 students reached by the census-takers, were church-members, and that out of the 2,321 students only 325 were not church-members or adherents. Of the 2818 students in attendance last year, only 576 were women. It is my belief that there is now less drinking among students at Ann Arbor than in any other University center in Europe or America where approximately near the same number of young men (there were more than 2,500 in Ann Arbor last year, counting those in the University, the University School of Music and the High School) are gathered together. The development of athletic interests, which are carefully looked after by a Committee of the Senate, and the new Waterman Gymnasium, furnish a vent for animal spirits that might otherwise spend themselves in dissipation. There is no "fast set;" plenty of "fast men" come, but they are either eliminated by the University authorities, or find the atmosphere uncongenial and withdraw before they give cause for action. In matters of discipline the authorities of a State University enjoy certain advantages the extent and significance of which are perhaps not generally appreciated.

pass by on the other side? What would be the proper course for a Christian church to pursue, with the spiritual interests of so many of its own children at stake?

IS THE STATE UNIVERSITY HERE TO STAY?

But a church must have regard for the future as well as for the present. The University of Michigan is one of a class. The question inevitably suggests itself: Are the state universities of sufficient stability to warrant the expenditure of effort and of funds, on the part of the church, to reach and help their students?

For historical reasons, which are so obvious that they do not need to be set forth, in the states along the northern seaboard colleges and universities of private endowment have had the field almost to themselves. But west of New York and Pennsylvania denominational institutions have no such foothold, while in at least three states the state university has so far outstripped all the other institutions of advanced education that under existing conditions they can never hope to catch up.[12] It may be that the University of Chicago will yet find a serious rival in the University of Illinois.[13] From present indications

[12] The total disbursements of the University of Michigan for the year 1894-5 amounted to $434,231.92, including only about $55,000 for permanent improvements; the enrollment of students was 2,818, not counting those who came to the Summer School.

The enrollment of the University of Minnesota in 1894-5 was 1,928, or with the Summer School students, 2,171; income (see the Catalogue, p. 11), $225,500.

The attendance at the University of Wisconsin in the same year was 1,520, or, including students of the Summer School, 1,671; total disbursements for the fiscal year ending September 30, 1894, $393,734.60, including, apparently, about $110,000 for permanent improvements.

In estimating the expenditure of several of the State Universities, account should be taken of the fact that the same amount of money is made to go further, particularly in the payment of salaries, than in the larger universities of private endowment situated in regions where living is more expensive.

[13] Extract from a letter from President Draper, dated 15 October, 1895: "The last Legislature made an appropriation of $424,000 for the purposes of the State University. Of this sum $150,000 was for a new library building, and $15,000 for an astronomical observatory."

the growth of a considerable group of the state universities bids fair to keep pace with the increase in population.[14] Our higher education is now in a process of differentiation and of rapid development. According to present tendencies, the university of the future will be an aggregation of schools for specialists, or professional schools, among which a philosophical faculty, represented to-day by the so-called graduate school, will hold a prominent place. After a time a full undergraduate course will be reckoned equally essential as a preparation for all advanced studies; and it is highly probable that this undergraduate instruction will be given by the larger city high schools, the courses of which will be extended and enriched,[15] as well as by the denominational colleges. In Chicago, for example, at the present time, a six-year high school course is open to all students; and our Michigan high schools occasionally conduct pupils over the work of the whole or a part of the freshman year. These are signs of the times. The undergraduate studies, which may easily be taught in many local centers, tend more and more to be distinguished from the higher or professional work of the university. As this differentiation goes on, and the proper work of the university is further developed, the cost of advanced instruction increases at an almost incredible rate, partly by reason of continual extension of the salary list, partly because of more ample and more expensive equipment in the way of books, laboratories and apparatus. The modern university methods in America, as in Germany, concentrate the work of the ablest professors upon relatively few students. In the

[14]The statistics given by Chancellor MacLean are surprising; see p. 32.

[15]The writer's views on this point were stated more in detail in an address on "The Future of the High School" (before a Conference of University and Preparatory Teachers at the University of Chicago, 15 November), published in an abridged form in the Educational Review for February, 1896; the educational position of the high school teacher is touched upon in a discussion which will appear in the School Review for September.

earlier instruction students can be taught almost wholly in larger groups or classes; but the more advanced the instruction the more individual it becomes, till one occasionally finds men of the first rank in ability and reputation giving their attention chiefly to a dozen men or less. Experience has shown that this is the sort of training that in the higher fields brings the best results, and there can never be a return to the methods of a half century ago. The expense of a working library and laboratory, or collection of illustrative material, is great for each of the many specialties; and with the extension of research along all lines the expense will continually increase.[16]

From these and other considerations which suggest themselves, it is evident that the cost of university instruction is no longer what it was twenty or even ten years ago. The time has already come when, from an educational point of view, several of the largest institutions of private endowment are hardly equal to the demands which press upon them. In the west, broadly speaking, the educational demands are in advance of the amassing of material resources. If the state universities did not exist, it is more than doubtful whether, in view of the rapid increase of population, it would have been possible for private generosity to meet the needs of advanced instruction. The early policy of the Congregationalists in planting denominational schools in the west as the frontier advanced is worthy of all praise. The results of it have been of incalculable value to

---

[16]President David J. Hill (article on "The Cost of Universities," in the Forum for November, 1889, pp. 297-304), says: "It is easy for any person who knows anything of the income and expenditures of our American institutions, to see from these data, not only that we have not any that correspond in kind to the universities of the highest grade in Germany, but that we never can have them without further enlargement of our conceptions of the magnitude and cost of such enterprises." * * * "In almost every American State there is some existing educational foundation which could be made the nucleus of a true university, and which is financially fit to receive and conserve large sums of money."

our country. In like manner the policy of the Presbyterian
church in establishing thorough schools in new regions where
society is just organizing itself, is to be commended as not only
far-seeing from a religious point of view, but also patriotic. But
as our states increase in population and resources, and the duty
of providing the highest education is fully recognized as impera-
tive, a true university will be required for every two or three
millions of inhabitants. In the larger number of instances this
university, from the cost of it, will of necessity be a state institution; and endowments for educational purposes, greater in
abundance and amount, will be given to state universities, on
account of the security of the investment.[17] The University of
Michigan has thus far received gifts amounting in the aggregate
to more than half a million dollars.[18] This does not include
gifts to university organizations, or organizations which have
no reason of being apart from the university, amounting to
$175,000.00 more.[19]

[17]See Table III., and President Angell's comments, p. 31.

[18]An itemized statement is given in The University Record, Vol.
IV., No. 4 (February, 1895), pp. 99 and 100.

Within the present year a law has been passed requiring the State
Treasurer of Michigan to receive endowment funds offered him for
the University, and to pay interest on them to the Treasurer of the
University; the principal being used for State purposes (so far dimin-
ishing the amounts to be raised by taxation), the State is bound to pay
the interest forever. This is the most secure and favorable investment of funds for educational purposes yet devised; it can not fail to
increase greatly the gifts of endowment funds to the University of
Michigan. The text of this law is given in The President's Report to
the Board of Regents for the year ending September 30, 1895, pp.
36, 37.

[19]Distributed as follows:

Students' Christian Association $40,000 00
Hobart Guild of the Episcopal Church.................... 85,000 00
Wesleyan Guild of the Methodist Church................. 8,000 00
Tappan Presbyterian Association 42,000 00

The Wesleyan Guild has purchased property, but has not yet
erected a building.

The largest gifts to the Tappan Presbyterian Association have
been as follows:

Mrs. H. Louise Doe Sackett, of Ann Arbor, real estate and
   residence $12,000 00
Hon. James McMillan, of Detroit, "McMillan Hall".......... 21,000 00
Library of the late Rev. Geo. Duffield, of Detroit....... 5,000 volumes
Library of the late Rev. Richard Atterbury............ 600 volumes

The library at McMillan Hall now contains 6,000 volumes.

Generally speaking, the financial foundation of the state universities, even in their present stage of development, is more secure than that of the institutions of private endowment; for their main income is not drawn from invested funds, which may be lost by unwise investment, or frittered away in meeting current expenses. Founded on the organic law of the commonwealth, and supported by taxation, they have their endowment in the resources of the whole people, from generation to generation.[20] Mischievous legislation may disturb them momentarily; but as our standards of intelligence and of political administration are raised, this possible source of harm will be eliminated. The state university will not be cast off by the people, because in the future, as now, it will be recognized as the logical continuation and completion of the system of public schools, which has been set as the corner-stone of our civic life, and must be regarded as fundamental to our civilization. From the primary school to the high school, from the high school to the university, will be the course of advancement in studies in the future, as to-day, though the lines of cleavage between the three parts of the same system will fall at different points. As the high school has already become our national type in secondary education, so the American university, which is slowly emerging into view, will, as a type, unquestionably be a state university. The academies, colleges and universities of private endowment, have, and are destined to have, a mission of the highest importance to society. No one who has analyzed the educational tendencies of the past decade can fail to be impressed with the rapidity with which our educational institutions are assuming a definite relation to one another and are settling into permanent and

---

[20] In Michigan the University receives each year, independently of special appropriations, a tax of 1-6 of a mill on all the taxable property of the State; the amount received from this source will increase with the increase of valuation. The support of the State University in several other States is guaranteed by a similar arrangement.

typical forms.[21]   Among them none have a firmer foundation than the state universities.   These have gained their position—not without earnest and persistent opposition—by reason of the logic of events; and one might as easily arrest their develop-ment as dam Niagara with autumn leaves.

THE CHURCH CONFRONTED WITH A CONDITION, NOT A THEORY.

At this point, believing that you, who are familiar with the conditions, will probably agree with me in regard to the per-manency and promise of the institutions for higher education supported by the states, I am sorely tempted to offer some ob-servations on the relation of the church to the state university; but I forbear.   You, brethren of the synod, are confronted with a condition, not a theory.   Believing that an educational modus vivendi between the religious denominations and the state uni-

---

[21]Some light on the questions suggested by the last statements may be gained from the following:

Martin, Supervisor G. H.: The Evolution of the Massachusetts Pub-lic School System. New York, 1894.

Angell, President James B.: State Universities in the West. Address before the Twenty-seventh Convocation of the University of the State of New York, 1889. In the Proceedings.

White, Andrew D.: The Future of American Universities. In the North American Review, Vol. 151 (1890), pp. 443-452.

Holst, Professor H. von: The Nationalization of Education and the Universities. In The Monist, Vol. 3 (1893), pp. 493-509.

Holst, Professor H. von: The Need of Universities in the United States. In The Educational Review, Vol. 5 (1893), pp. 105-119.

Butler, Professor N. M.: Introduction to Perry's Translation of Paul-sen's German Universities. New York, 1895.

Angell, President James B.: State Universities. Address at the Dedication of Academic Hall and the new Department Building at the University of Missouri, 4 June, 1895. Columbia, Missouri. Published by the University, 1895.

versity is possible, and not so very difficult of realization, [22] I do not wish at this time to obscure the facts by a discussion of principles. It is important to realize that the foundations of the state universities are secure, that their influence is becoming every year a larger factor in the culture of the whole country and of the world,[23] and that at the present time our State

---

[22] Valuable contributions to the literature of this subject are the following:

Pierson, Rev. A. T., with Rev. J. A. Wight, Rev. H. P. Collin, Rev. Job Pierson and Elders W. J. Baxter, E. A. Frazer and A. J. Aldrich, forming a special committee of Synod: The Synod of Michigan and the State University. In the Minutes of the Synod of Michigan, 1882 (6 pp.).

Frieze, Professor Henry S.: The Relations of the State University to Religion. Address before the graduating classes of the University of Michigan in 1887. In The Semi-Centennial Celebration of the Organization of the University of Michigan. [Ann Arbor. Published. by the University, 1888], pp. 17-54. Also, printed in pamphlet form.

Angell, President James B.: Religious Life in Our State Universities. In the Andover Review, Vol. 13 (1890), pp. 365-372.

D'Ooge, Professor Martin L.: The Religious Life of the University. In Religious Thought at the University of Michigan. Being addresses delivered at the Sunday morning services of the Students' Christian Association. [Ann Arbor, 1893, pp. xii., 247], pp. viii.-xii.

Ely, Professor Richard T.: The Universities and the Churches. Address before the Thirty-first Convocation of the University of the State of New York, 1893. Albany. University of the State of New York.

Updike, Rev. Eugene G.: Christianity and the State University. A Sermon delivered at the First Congregational Church, Madison, Wis. Madison. Published by the Christian Associations of the University of Wisconsin, 1894.

Ely, Professor Richard T.: The Higher Education and the Churches. In The Kingdom (Minneapolis), 7 June, 1895.

Ely, Professor Richard T.: State Universities. In The Cosmopolitan for October, 1895.

[23] The general or cosmopolitan character of the attendance at the University of Michigan is noteworthy. Last year about 55 per cent. (1,551) of the 2,818 students were residents of Michigan. Of the 1,267 students from outside the State, 300 came from Illinois, 200 from Ohio, and 109 from Indiana; Pennsylvania stands fifth on the list with 85 students, New York sixth, with 73. Not to mention in detail the num-

University is the largest of its class; but it is more vital to the interests represented here to-day to grasp the fact that the second largest Presbyterian college in the United States, in point of numbers, is at this moment a part of the University of Michigan. It would be more than a mere waste of breath to say, "Let the Presbyterian students go to Presbyterian institutions;" the number increases year by year. Presbyterian tax-payers give their full share toward the support of the state universities. Their sons and daughters will continue to take advantage of the educational opportunities which are open to them by right, not by sufferance, nor as a matter of patronage.

What shall the Presbyterian church do for the Presbyterian students at Ann Arbor? This question is of course somewhat concerned with that more remote future, when the University shall have become purely professional in its work and aims; but it demands solution at once for the students, undergraduate and professional, that are on the ground now, and for the thousands that will follow in their footsteps during the next few years.

The chief danger to student life in the collegiate and university period lies not, as so often assumed, in the tendency of those naturally weak or wayward to be led astray by evil companions; it lies in the fact that the highest and best minds, the most earnest and candid souls, are from their devotion to the

---

ber coming from more distant Western States and Territories ("every State in the Union is represented except Nevada"), Massachusetts and the Province of Ontario furnished each the same number, 23; from New Hampshire came 7, from Maine, New Jersey and North Carolina, each 4, from Texas 11, from Vermont, the District of Columbia, Florida, Louisiana and Oklahoma, each 3; from Maryland, Virginia and West Virginia, each 2; from Connecticut and Rhode Island, 1 each. Foreign countries were represented as follows: Germany 5, China 4, England 3; Mexico, Province of Quebec, New Brunswick, Scotland, and Switzerland, each 2; and the Argentine Republic, Barbadoes, Bulgaria, Italy, Japan, South Africa, Sweden, each 1. The full summary by States and by departments is given in the Calendar for 1894-95, pp. 295-296.

pursuit of knowledge liable to experience a deadening of the spiritual consciousness. Those students in whom is revealed the most marked capacity for large service to humanity, may thus go forth with the highest part of their natures undeveloped, lacking that spiritual force which multiplies ten-fold the influence of every kind of ability for good work in the world. Intensity of intellectual life, from the very juxtaposition of minds interested in many fields of thought, but all bent upon like ends, seems to increase with the size of universities. Time alone will tell whether, after taking into account all antecedent and immediate conditions, students in great institutions of private endowment are less subject to this atrophy of the spiritual nature than those in state universities of the same size. Freedom of research must and will be maintained. But it seems to have escaped the notice of many that no form of endowment has yet been devised that will guarantee the presentation of truth or doctrine from precisely the same point of view from one century to another;[24] and that, on the other hand, there is no apparent reason why a university supported by tax-payers, the great majority of whom believe in Christianity, should necessarily be hostile to Christianity in the tone of its instruction.

Experience has shown, it seems to me, that the remedy to meet this defect in advanced education, to offset the tendencies that make for the effacement of the spiritual life, cannot be found in the activity of the local churches in university towns, no matter how earnest and efficient they may be. It must lie in teaching, not so much in the teaching of religion as in the teaching of the Bible; and that, too, from the English form as a starting point. It is not enough to give courses in Hellenistic Greek

[24]Numerous and cogent illustrations of the fate of restrictive religious endowments will occur to anyone familiar with the history of education. The subject is touched upon by Dr. J. G. Fitch in a paper on "Endowments," in the Proceedings of the Second Annual Convention of the College Association of Pennsylvania, 1888, pp. 20-50.

and in Hebrew, as the University now does, with the minute study of portions of the Scriptures in those tongues. These courses from the nature of the case are available for only a small number of students, and are linguistic in their scope. Courses should be offered which will undertake the interpretation of the Bible as literature, as history and as philosophy. Into them should go a scholarship second to that of no other chair, expressed through the medium of a warm and earnest spiritual nature. This proposition needs neither amplification nor justification before you. The careful avoidance of the Bible in courses of instruction, cutting off from those interested in it the possibility of a scientific study of it under a master of intellectual grasp and standing, may well leave upon the student the impression that the Book of Books is after all only a matter for ministers and Sunday School children.

This instruction in the Bible cannot be, and ought not to be, given at the expense of the state. This proposition, as the other, needs only to be stated to be accepted by you. But that a church has a right to offer to its own student members and adherents, grouped in any center, such instruction in the Bible as it may deem expedient, no one will for a moment question. Whether a part of this instruction, when elected and taken as any other study by those already in a State University, can be made of such a character that it may properly receive credit on the records of the University towards a diploma, is a question that need not be raised here; it belongs to the category of questions that can be settled only after both deliberation and experiment. It is perhaps worth while to add that nowhere else will the conditions be found more favorable for working out the problem of giving religious instruction to the students of a State University than at Ann Arbor; and that, as the eyes of other State Universities are fixed upon the University of Michigan, a happy solution of the problem here would be of inestimable value to the religious interests of kindred institutions.

It is surprising that the Presbyterian Church did not long ago recognize Ann Arbor as a strategic point of the highest importance, that the Church has remained blind to her own interests in this matter.[25] Does the Church need ministers? Let her come and get them, by placing the claims of the ministry before students of her own nurturing, who are bright in mind and quick of sympathy, who are halting between opinions regarding their choice of a life-work. Let the Church put a tide-mill in this channel, and generate a spiritual force that will be felt in every part of our country. Here can be grasped, in a single hand, a network of influence that will reach out in every direction to limits that no man can reckon. The students are here! They do not need to be driven in from highways and byways, and coaxed and coddled into an education. A manlier, stronger collection of students, in brain and character, does not anywhere exist. These lives, fresh in their enthusiasm and hope, are dynamos; let the Church lend to them a motive power and they will send a spiritual thrill to the uttermost parts of the earth.

Upon you, Brethren, of the Synod of Michigan, rests the weight of a grave responsibility. This Synod has more than once put itself on record regarding the importance of the work at Ann Arbor. As a layman, and one approaching the subject from an educational point of view, it is not for me to remind you, so many of whom are clergymen, of your duty. The Presbyterian Church in Michigan has been blessed beyond her sister churches in material resources and in the number of highly educated and powerful men enlisted in her ministry; probably no

---

[25] The conclusion arrived at by Mr. Wilcox, after some months of work collecting the testimony and statistics presented on pp. 36-43, is emphatic and well worth recording; see p. 33.

other ecclesiastical body in the State is at present capable of wielding a greater influence. For the good—I do not say of the Church, for that is too narrow a view—for the good of humanity, for the cause that makes for righteousness in the world, this work must be strengthened by you. Time and again you have heard from our pastor at Ann Arbor that a struggling church in a small city, without a wealthy membership, can not possibly provide for the needs of this array of Presbyterian students. You know also that the work is utterly beyond the reach of professors, whose hands are full with the exacting requirements of university specialties. You have been informed that the generosity of friends has provided a building suitable for the work, and the nucleus of a library; you have more than once been reminded that the self-sacrificing help of a few brethren in the ministry has made it possible to do a small work in a small, hand-to-mouth way, yet with most gratifying results. And our needs are known to you. The amount of two thousand dollars a year, or an endowment producing that sum, for current expenses, is a very small matter for a Synod with resources such as this Synod has. But above all else, send us a man! Station at Ann Arbor the man of largest intellect, the most scholarly man, the man with most profound knowledge of the Bible as a specialty, the man of broadest sympathies and of deepest spirituality, that can be found anywhere. Let his courses in the Bible be just as scholarly, just as thorough, just as inspiring and scientifically strong as any course offered by a university professor anywhere. Pay such a man whatever may be necessary; what is a salary of $3,000 or $5,000 a year in comparison with the importance of the work, or when measured by the expenditures of our Church in other fields? But do not longer delay, while the golden opportunity to cherish and mould the Church's own in this center, so full of intellectual vitality, is slipping away. Resolutions of commendation are pleasant enough, but the time has now come for action.

During the six years of my connection with the University of Michigan, I have heard a good deal about the interest of the Synod of Michigan in the work concerning which I have spoken. I ask you frankly, What tangible evidence is there of it? If Presbyterian students come to Ann Arbor from your churches, and from the churches of your brethren in other states and countries, and are there weaned from the things of the spirit, and through an unsymmetrical development let the training of intellect choke out the spiritual life, if so they make shipwreck of their careers, their blood will be required at your hands. Some day the Church will awaken to the significance of all this. The Presbyterian Church moves slowly, but when once it goes forward it moves with the irresistible momentum of a profound conviction. Some day the Church will stand before you with downcast face, and with a voice of ineffable sadness will say, "Men of the Synod of Michigan, when you had in your midst this precious, precious charge, why did you not tell me? Why did you not pursue me until, as the unjust judge, I turned and rendered justice to your cause? Why did you feed to my beloved children the husks of commendatory resolutions when they needed the Living Bread to sustain the spiritual life?" Confronted thus, will you have the shadow of an excuse to offer in justification of your indifference and neglect?

TABLE I.

SUMMARY OF CALLING-LIST OF PRESBYTERIAN STUDENTS AT THE UNIVERSITY OF MICHIGAN, COMPILED BY MR. B. H. KROEZE, STUDENT-SECRETARY OF THE TAPPAN PRESBYTERIAN ASSOCIATION, 1 OCTOBER TO 30 DECEMBER, 1894:

Department of Literature, Science and the Arts—

	Men.	Women.	Total.
Members of the Presbyterian Church	112	68	
Students of Presbyterian preference	62	15	
	174	83	257

Department of Law—

Members of the Presbyterian Church	40	1	
Of Presbyterian preference	27	0	
	67	1	68

Department of Medicine and Surgery—

Members of the Presbyterian Church	30	4	
Of Presbyterian preference	17	1	
	47	5	52

Department of Dental Surgery—

Members of the Presbyterian Church	12	1	
Of Presbyterian preference	5	0	
	17	1	18

Department of Pharmacy—

Members of the Presbyterian Church	2	0	
Of Presbyterian preference	4		
	6		6
	311	90	401

Mr. Kroeze's list contained also the names of 49 Presbyterian students in the Ann Arbor High School, distributed as follows:

	Boys.	Girls.	
Members of the Presbyterian Church	21	8	
Of Presbyterian preference	14	6	
	35	14	49

On the list were the names of 25 University students who attended no church regularly, but came to the Presbyterian Church as often as to any.................................. 25

The total number of students registered by Mr. Kroeze in the three months and considered by him properly under the care of the Church was, therefore 475

TABLE II.

AVERAGE COST TO THE BOARD AND TO THE CHURCH OF
STUDENTS IN AIDED INSTITUTIONS WHICH
HAVE COLLEGE STUDENTS, 1894-95.[26]

Institutions 1894-95.	Collegiate Students.	Other Students.	Contributed by College Board.	Average per Student.	Contributed by Churches, Etc.	Total Contributed, Average per Student.	Total Average per Student.
Albany, Oregon ..	27	106	$1,400	$10.52	$ 201	$ 1.51	$12.03
Albert Lea, Minn..	13	37	500	10.00	1,727	34.54	44.54
Alma, Michigan ...	38	117	....	....	6,296	40.61	40.61
Bellevue, Neb	21	66	1,250	14.36	1.142	13.12	27.48
Coates, Ind.......	25	93	1,000	8.47	23,030	195.24	203.71
Emporia, Kas	70	40	1,000	9.09	7,587	68.97	78.06
Dubuque, Iowa ...	32	7	800	2.05	1,506	39.39	41.44
Greenville & T.Tenn	42	116	500	3.16	421	2.66	5.82
Hastings, Neb.. ..	30	52	1,250	15.24	2,480	30.24	45.48
Montana	22	58	1,000	12.50	8,153	101.91	114.41
Occidental, Cal....	21	52	1,000	13.69	2,687	36.80	50.49
Oswego, Kas	36	19	750	13.63	729	13.25	26.88
Pierre, S. D........	11	72	1,000	12.04	637	7.55	19.59
Washington, Tenn .	46	84	500	3.84	2,082	16.01	19.85
Southwest, Col.. ..	14	45	500	8.47	1,666	28.23	36.70
Whitworth, Wash .	42	25	1,200	17.91	162	2.41	20.32
Brookfield, Mo.. ..	24	154	500	2.75	1,000	5.50	8.25
Buena Vista, Ia....	9	104	800	7.07	2,057	18.20	25.27
Gale, Wis..	7	65	....	....	1,391	19.31	19.31
Glen Rose, Tex....	4	47	800	15.68	405	9.90	25.58
Lewis, Kas...	2	293	2,000	6.82	566	1.89	8.71
Princeton, Ky.. ...	52	58	650	5.90	1,007	9.15	15.05
	588	1.710	$18.400	$ 8.00	$66,941	$24.78	$32.78
Total		2,298					

The following amounts were contributed on payment of old indebtedness or to erect buildings, and should be deducted from the amount
contributed by churches, etc., to arrive at the amount of contributions
for current expenses:

Coates, Ind..............	$20,000	$25.75	$34.22
Emporia, Kas...........	5,000	23.51	32.60
Montana	6,000	26.91	39.41
Occidental, Cal.......	1,000	23.08	36.77
Washington, Tenn.....	1,500	4.47	8.31
Deduct $33,500, leaving.............	$33,441	$10.20	$18.28

[26]Compare also the Eleventh Annual Report of the Board of Aid for
Colleges and Academies of the Presbyterian Church, Chicago, 1894.

TABLE III.

PRIVATE GIFTS TO SEVERAL STATE UNIVERSITIES UP TO
THE BEGINNING OF THE COLLEGIATE
YEAR, 1895-96.[27]

University of California, at Berkeley.......		$1,957,305.00
University of Colorado, at Boulder......·...		26,432.66
University of Indiana, at Bloomington:		
From Monroe County	$ 50,000.00	50,000.00
University of Minnesota, at Minneapolis...		154,566.81[28]
University of Missouri, at Columbia:		
From Boone County	257,000.00	
From the A. W. Collins fund.......	40,000.00	297,000.00[29]
Ohio State University, at Columbus:		
From Franklin County	300,000.00	
From individuals	201,000.00	501,000.00
University of Oregon, at Eugene..........		73,000.00
University of South Dakota, at Vermillion..		47,079.57
University of Texas, at Austin............		95,000.00
West Virginia University, at Morgantown..		51,000.00
University of Wisconsin, at Madison.:......		84,400.00[30]

[27]See The University Record, Vol. IV., No. 4 (February, 1895), pp.
97-100.

[28]In addition to various scholarship funds and prizes, the income of
which is available, the principal not yet having been turned over to
the University. Other gifts also "have been made to the University,
but not yet become available."

[29]Also "The James S. Rollins scholarship fund being 5 per cent
upon $6,000.00."

[30]After these figures were published, gifts amounting to $180,000.00,
to the University of Kansas, at Lawrence, were reported.

PRESIDENT ANGELL ON GIFTS TO STATE UNIVERSITIES.

In regard to the figures given in Table III., President Angell remarks:

"There are at least three reasons why the State Universities have not been so generously aided by private munificence as could be desired.

"First, they are found in the younger States, where wealth has not been accumulated so largely as in the East, and where all the capital has been needed in the development of industries.

"Secondly, there was serious mismanagement in the earlier history of most of the State Universities. The lands given by the United States were in many cases sold at too low prices, so that the original endowment was largely sacrificed. Bitter controversies arose too often over the conduct of the affairs of the institutions. These facts discouraged generous men from giving to them. They doubted whether endowments which they might make would be cared for and prudently and efficiently managed.

"Thirdly, as the States increased in wealth and appropriated funds with some liberality to their Universities, not a few men of wealth excused themselves from making donations to those institutions by affirming that the States were rich enough to furnish all the help needed.

"But the figures given above furnish gratifying evidence that the former reluctance of large-hearted men and women to contribute to the strengthening of State Universities is rapidly disappearing. When we remember how young are some of the institutions named, we must regard the showing as very creditable and encouraging. We have no doubt that henceforth important gifts to them will be much more frequent. For there can no longer be any doubt that the State Universities are here to stay, and that with probably one or two exceptions the State University is to be the strongest and most important University in each State west of New York and Pennsylvania. The old questioning about their merits and their probable duration has come to an end. The States have put too much money into the plant to think of abandoning them. By accepting grants of lands they have put themselves under bonds to cherish the Universities. The work which these institutions have done and are doing, so much larger and more varied than that of the ordinary incorporated college in the West, valuable as that is, has commended them to the public, which could not now be persuaded to dispense with them.

"The States have so fully evinced their determination to maintain them that the stability of their existence may be said to be assured. Moreover, the years of experience which the authorities of them have had in conducting them have enabled the regents or trustees to inspire the public with confidence in the wisdom and steadiness of their management.

"Therefore, we cannot but believe that men and women of means will give much more freely in the future to the State Universities than they have given in the past."

CHANCELLOR MACLEAN ON THE GROWTH OF THE STATE UNIVERSITIES.[31]

"The increase in the attendance upon these universities is perhaps unparalleled in the annals of education. The total number of students in eight representative State Universities (California, Illinois, Iowa, Kansas, Michigan, Minnesota, Nebraska, Wisconsin) in the year 1885 was 4,230, in the year 1895 the number was 13,500, an increase of 320 per cent. It is gratifying to note that our own University has increased from 373 students in 1885 to 1,550 students in 1895, a percentage of increase of 400 per cent, something unsurpassed except by Minnesota's unheard of increase of 777 per cent.

"The increase in the same period in eight New England Colleges and Universities (Amherst, Bowdoin, Brown, Dartmouth, Harvard, Williams, Wesleyan, Yale) is 20 per cent. The increase in eight representative denominational colleges (Beloit, Carleton, Cornell, Hillsdale, Iowa College, Lawrence, Ripon, St. John's) in the States of Michigan, Wisconsin, Minnesota and Iowa, is 14¼ per cent. From these statistics it is evident that not the ratio of population or material causes account for the gain of the State Universities. Among the many causes contributing to the increase are the development of State High Schools, the enlarged wealth of the State, and, above all, the removal of the fears and prejudices of the people concerning the Universities. The prac-

---

[31]From the inaugural address of Chancellor MacLean, 14 February, 1896, as reported in the Nebraska State Journal of 15 February.

tical nationalization of education in the public school system has convinced the people of the patriotic design and necessity of the entire system, including the Universities. They have passed the experimental stage."

THE DUTY OF THE CHURCHES TO THE STATE UNIVERSITY.

"What attitude," says Mr. Wilcox, approaching the subject from the point of view of a student of Social Science, "shall the churches assume toward the State University? The higher institutions of learning will not furnish the churches with a ministry unless the churches are willing to adjust themselves to the new conditions of life which present-day developments in science and industry have brought about. The Church can save its life only by growth. A religion that is true for the life-needs of to-day, will hold its own on the open field. To say that the institutions of the people are irreligious is simply to concede that the churches have no grip on the people who make the institutions; and to withdraw the forces of religion from these institutions is to admit that the battle has gone against Christianity, and that its mission henceforth must not be to save society, but to save the Church. If religion is to be an active, aggressive force among men, why not make the centers of the life of men the centers of religious effort?

"In a letter from Rev. Charles Dunlap, University of Michigan, Class of 1855, are these words:

"'In later years the churches withdrew their students for the ministry from the University, and sent them, as they have done in this State (Iowa) in the Presbyterian Church, to smaller colleges of their own. This has been, in my opinion, a mistake. It has withdrawn a good deal of the religious influence from the State institutions, where it was needed, and brought about the condition of which they complain.'

"The fact is that we have State Universities and denominational Colleges coming into competition; there is no hope that the State will ever withdraw from so critical and extensive a portion of the educational field as that occupied by collegiate work. In the face of these conditions, what are the churches to do for their own best interests? It appears to me that they should be in no haste to found any more small colleges in fields already occupied; they should not discourage attendance at State Universities; but they should devote a fair share of their energies and funds to the strengthening of Christian influences at those centers of educational life."

STATISTICS

BEARING UPON

Religious and Moral Tendencies

AT THE

UNIVERSITY OF MICHIGAN

By DELOS F. WILCOX

I.—THE CONTRIBUTIONS OF THE UNIVERSITY OF MICHIGAN TO THE MINISTRY AND MISSION FIELDS.

In the preparation of the following statistics, I have used as sources of information the General Catalogue of 1890, Chase's University Book of 1880, correspondence with alumni, and personal knowledge of the last years. Owing to the limitations of space, a large part of the matter collected is not given. I have aimed to present only that which seemed most important.

In reckoning percentages of clergymen, I have taken the number of male classical graduates as a basis, because the candidates for the ministry in the later years, as in the earlier, nearly always took the B. A. course; while the other degrees pretty nearly represent the widening of collegiate education to take in those engaged in other‚ lines of work, formerly unrepresented in college circles.

Table IV. shows the number and percentage of clergymen from each of the first fifty graduating classes, as correctly as I have been able to ascertain. There are reckoned in this list a few who died while pursuing theological studies, or before they had fairly started in the ministry; a few, who since leaving the theological seminary, have given most of their time to educational work; and a few who entered the ministry with seemingly very little preparation in the way of formal theological study.

Table V. shows the number and percentages of the graduates from 1845 to 1880 who have entered the ministry, law, teaching, and business. The facts for the years since 1880 are too unsettled to be of much value. It often takes a good many years for a college graduate to find his place in the world.

Table VI. gives the places at which the clergymen of the first thirty-six classes received their theological training.

In Tables VII. and VIII. the numbers of clergymen attending the seminaries of the different denominations are given.

Table IX. shows the distribution of missionaries from the University of Michigan in the various fields, the number of graduates and non-graduates, and the number of each sex.

Table X. gives a statistical summary of the religious workers who have gone out from the University.

TABLE IV.

CLERGYMEN AMONG THE CLASSICAL GRADUATES OF THE FIRST FIFTY CLASSES.

Class.	No. of B. A. Male Graduates.	No. of B. A. Clergymen.	Percentages.	Clergymen with other degrees.
1845	12	2	16.7	
1846	17	3	17.6	
1847	12	2	16.7	
1848	16	4	25.0	
1849	24	9	37.5	
1850	12	3	25.0	
1851	10	2	20.0	
1852	10	4	40.0	
1853	11	2	18.2	
1854	21	4	19.0	
1845-1854	145	35	24.1	
1855	15	6	40.0	
1856	20	2	10.0	
1857	28	10	35.7	
1858	30	4	13.3	
1859	27	2	7.4	2
1860	21	4	19.0	
1861	37	5	13.5	
1862	37	6	16.2	
1863	23	1	4.3	
1864	22	3	13.6	
1855-1864	260	43	16.6	2
1865	21	4	19.0	
1866	32	4	12.5	1
1867	26	7	27.0	1
1868	35	2	5.7	
1869	23	3	13.0	
1870	42	5	11.9	1
1871	36	6	16.7	
1872	57	10	17.5	
1873	40	3	7.5	
1874	31	3	9.7	1
1865-1874	343	47	13.7	4
1875	38	3	8.0	
1876	32	1	3.1	1
1877	33	2	6.1	1
1878	33	1	3.0	1
1879	33	2	6.1	
1880	33	2	6.0	
1881	48	2	4.2	
1882	37	1	2.7	1
1883	46	2	4.7	
1884	43	6	13.6	1
1875-1884	376	22	5.9	5

TABLE IV.—*Continued.*

Class	No. of B. A. Male Graduates,	No. of B A. Clergymen.	Percentages	Clergymen with other degrees.
1885	34	1	3.2	1
1886	43	1	2.3	
1887	32	4	12.5	
1888	39	5	12.8	2
1889	23	0	00.0	1
1890	36	1	2.8	
1891	39	4	10.2	1
1892	45	4	8.9	1
1893	49	5	10.2	1
1894	46	7	15.2	3
1885-1894	386	32	8.3	10
1845-1894	1510	179	11.9	21

TABLE V.

RELATIVE PROPORTION OF CLERGYMEN, LAWYERS, TEACH-
ERS AND BUSINESS MEN, 1845-1880.

CLASSES.	B. A. Male Gradu- tes.	CLERGYMEN. No.	Per cent.	LAWYERS, No.	Per cent.	TEACHERS. No.	Per cent.	BUSINESS MEN. No.	Per cent
1845-1854	145	35	24.1	61	42.1	17	11.7	14	9.7
1855-1864	260	43	16.6	86	33.2	54	20.8	24	9.3
1865-1874	343	47	13.7	130	38.1	66	19.4	49	14.4
1875-1880	202	11	5.5	52	26.0	50	25.0	34	17.0
1845-1880	950	136	14.3	329	34.8	187	19.8	121	13.9

TABLE VI.

THEOLOGICAL SEMINARY TRAINING, 1845-1880.

Attended no Seminary, or seminary not ascertained....	48
Union ..	26
Auburn ..	17
Chicago ..	9
Princeton ..	7
Andover · ..	6
General	6
Yale	4
Newton	3
Kalamazoo	2
Rochester	2
Harvard Divinity School	2
Nashotah	2
Protestant Episcopal Theological Seminary of Virginia..	1
Westminster, Presbyterian	1
Seabury Divinity School	1
Lane	1
Meadville	1
Brunswick, N. J., Reformed Church.	1
Oberlin ..	1
Newburgh	1
Garrett Biblical Institute	1
Cumberland	1
Baptist Union, Morgan Park, Ill.	1
Total	145

TABLE VII.

DISTRIBUTION OF CLERGYMEN FROM CLASSES OF 1845-1880 BY DENOMINATIONS OF THE SEMINARIES.

Presbyterian Seminaries	54
Congregational Seminaries	20
Protestant Episcopal Seminaries	10
Baptist Seminaries	8
Unitarian Seminaries	3
Methodist Seminaries	1
Reformed Church Seminaries	1
Total	97
No Seminary, or Seminary not ascertained	48
Total	145

TABLE VIII.

DISTRIBUTION OF CLERGYMEN FROM CLASSES OF 1845-1880 BY DENOMINATIONS.

Presbyterian	38
Methodist	30
Congregational	21
Baptist	13
Protestant Episcopal	12
Lutheran	2
Reformed Church	1
Unknown	28
Total	145

TABLE IX.

MISSIONARIES FROM THE UNIVERSITY OF MICHIGAN.

China	20
Turkey	7
India	6
Japan	4
Africa	3
Burmah	3
Corea	2
Mexico	2
Hawaiian Islands	2
Italy	2
Bulgaria	2
Syria	1
Siam	1
Alaska	1
Indians	1
Total	57

DISTRIBUTION OF MISSIONARIES BY DEPARTMENTS.

Graduates from Department of Medicine	36
Graduates from Department of Literature, Science and the Arts	14
Non-graduates	7
Total	57

TABLE IX.—*Continued.*

DISTRIBUTION OF MISSIONARIES ACCORDING TO SEX.

Men 28
Women 29
                          ___
*Total 57

TABLE X.

RELIGIOUS WORKERS FROM THE UNIVERSITY OF MICHIGAN,
1845-1894.

Classical Graduate clergymen 179
Other literary graduate clergymen..................... 21
Non-graduate and higher degree clergymen[32]............ 52
Medical missionaries 36
Other missionaries, not included above................ 11
                                                     ___
    Total 299

II.—THE STUDENTS' CHRISTIAN ASSOCIATION.

"The most active and potent religious influence in the University," says Prof. D'Ooge,[33] "has emanated from the organization known as the Students' Christian Association. This society recently celebrated the thirty-fifth anniversary of its founding, and is now aknowledged to be the oldest association of its kind in this country. It started on its career under the most prevalent and thorough religious awakening that has ever come to bless the life of the University, an awakening that was born of the general revival that swept over all our land in 1857 and 1858. About 1872 it took charge of all religious work in the University, organized prayer-meetings, instituted Bible classes, and sought to develop the missionary spirit and interest in the work of the ministry by organizing 'Mission' and 'Ministerial Bands.' The religious life of the student community was considerably stirred by a spiritual awakening which occurred in the winter of 1875.

"Meanwhile the Christian Association has enlarged the scope of its usefulness by conducting mission schools in and about the city, by holding religious services in the hospitals, and by assisting newly arrived students in finding desirable quarters for residence. With all the good work thus accomplished by this religious body," adds Prof. D'Ooge, writing in 1893, "it still remains true that for some reason the interest and sympathy of the student community, as a whole, have not been enlisted in this association and its objects to the extent that might have been expected."

---

[32]This list is probably very incomplete.
[33]"Religious Thought at the University of Michigan," pp. ix., x.

The Students' Christian Association occupied its fine building, New-berry Hall, in 1891. In 1883 the Young Men's Christian Association basis had been adopted, making evangelical church membership a condition for active membership in the Students' Christian Association. In 1892-1893 after much discussion, the whole membership basis was changed. The purpose of the Association was embodied in Article II. of the Constitu-tion, as follows: "The purpose of this Association is to lead men to an earnest study of the Scriptures; to a renunciation of sin; to a knowledge of Jesus Christ as their Divine Lord and Savior; to the acceptance of His words and the Holy Spirit as the guide of life; and to the cultiva-tion of Christian fellowship." Each candidate for active membership was required to sign the following pledge: "So far accepting the aim of this Association that I can work in harmony with its members, I agree to abide by its laws and seek its prosperity; I desire that my life be guided by the spirit of faith, prayer, and love which animated the life of Jesus Christ; I will cultivate with my associates a Christian friendship and sympathy, and will ever strive to help them to a knowl-edge of God and to a realization of the spiritual possibilities of the Christian life." This membership basis was considered too broad by some, and in May, 1895, after the organization of a College Young Men's Christian Association under the influence of John R. Mott, the Students' Christian Association changed its basis by simplifying the pledge to read thus: "Accepting the purpose of this Association, I agree to abide by its laws and seek its prosperity."

While the Students' Christian Association does not measure the re-ligious life of the University in its full extent, this Association is still the chief center of Christian work among the students.[14] Its member-ship for the past six years has been as follows:

1889-1890	411
1890-1891	422
1891-1892	435
1892-1893	556
1893-1894	478
1894-1895	375[15]

The membership of the Association is drawn chiefly from Presby-terians, Methodists, Congregationalists and Baptists. The decrease shown in the numbers during the last year is accounted for, to some extent, by the more careful weeding out of merely nominal members.

In 1892 and 1894 religious censuses of the students were taken, that in the latter year being too incomplete to be of statistical value. The following tables will show the most important results obtained:

---

[14]During the school year 1894-95 the Students' Christian Association conducted on the average about 16 religious services each week, in-cluding department prayer-meetings, class prayer-meetings, meetings of classes organized for the study of the Bible, and a general service on Sunday.

[15]Approximately.

TABLE XI.

RELIGIOUS CENSUS OF THE UNIVERSITY OF MICHIGAN,
1892-1893.

MEN.

Department.	Church Members.	Church Adherents.	Not Adherents.	Un-reached.	Total.
Literary	477	240	127	134	978
Law	214	169	101	154	638
Medical	120	84	34	35	273
Dental	57	48	22	55	182
Pharmacy	22	23	13	18	76
Homeopathic	25	13	7	5	50
Grand Total	915	577	304	401	2,197

WOMEN.

Department.	Church Members.	Church Adherents.	Not Adherents.	Un-reached.	Total.
Literary	334	101	16	62	513
Law	1	..	..	..	1
Medical	43	2	4	22	71
Dental	6	1	..	..	7
Pharmacy	1	3	..	2	6
Homeopathic	10	2	1	..	13
Grand Total	395	109	21	86	611

SUMMARY.

Department.	Church Members.	Church Adherents.	Not Adherents.	Un-reached.	Total.
Literary	811	341	143	196	1,491
Law	215	169	101	154	639
Medical	163	86	38	57	344
Dental	63	49	22	55	189
Pharmacy	23	26	13	20	82
Homeopathic	35	15	8	5	63
University......	1,310	686	325	487	[302]2.808

[302]This number includes 30 duplicates, where students were registered in more than one department. It was impossible to eliminate
these duplicates from the statistics. The actual registration in the
University, exclusive of duplicates, was 2,778.

TABLE XII.

PERCENTAGES OF STUDENTS REACHED WHO WERE CHURCH MEMBERS.

Department.	Men.	Women.	All.
Literary	57.2	74.1	62.6
Law	44.2	100.0	44.3
Medical	50.4	87.8	58.8
Dental	44.9	85.7	49.6
Pharmacy	37.9	25.0	37.1
Homeopathic	55.6	76.9	60.3
University	50.9	75.2	56.4

TABLE XIII.

DISTRIBUTION AMONG DENOMINATIONS.

Church.	Members.	Adherents.	Total.
Methodist	256	172	428
Presbyterian	264	143	407
Congregational	178	109	287
Protestant Episcopal	169	71	240
Baptist	134	30	164
Unitarian	40	95	135
Roman Catholic	88	5	93
Disciples of Christ	50	17	67
German Lutheran	26	1	27
Seventh Day Advent	23	1	24
Jewish	15	9	24
Universalist	5	12	17
Mormon	15	2	17
Reformed Church	9	4	13
Friends	9	2	11
English Lutheran	8	1	9
Miscellaneous	21	12	33
Total	1,310	686	1,996

TABLE XIV.

DISTRIBUTION OF SEVEN LEADING DENOMINATIONS BY DEPARTMENTS.

Church.	Lit.	Law.	Med.	Dent.	Phar.	Hom.	Univ.
Methodist	215	97	53	34	14	15	428
Presbyterian	234	79	50	19	13	12	407
Congregational	203	32	33	15	3	1	287
Protestant Episcopal	155	42	22	11	7	3	240
Baptist	101	25	19	8	2	9	164
Roman Catholic	40	29	18	3	1	2	93
Unitarian	98	20	11	5	1	0	135

www.ingramcontent.com/pod-product-compliance
Lightning Source LLC
Chambersburg PA
CBHW021549270326
41930CB00008B/1435